to appointments. Begin with the have", "I always", etc.

Some examples: I have all that I need in order to succeed. I am motivated. I am a money maker. I am powerful. My clients want to hear from me. I am able to do amazing things.

- <u>Write down your GOALS</u>. These have to be SMART (Specific, Measurable, Attainable, Realistic, Timely). Write your goal out 3-5 times. My BOLD coach had us write out one goal 10 times each day.

Some examples: I am on my 10th contract signed by June 1st. I will complete a BOLD 100 at least once this week. I will reach out to my entire database by the first of June.

- <u>Things I Did Well</u>. Write down a few successes. Celebrate your big wins. No big wins? Write down things you did, but didn't want to do. Some days "I got out of bed" is better than the alternative. Celebrate all wins.

- <u>Things I Learned</u>. At the end of each day, write down a few examples on the left side of your journal. Any lessons learned you experienced should be captured. Come back to these often.

- <u>Growth Plan</u>. You're either growing or your dying. There is no maintaining status quo. Write down 3-4 growth events each month in your journal. Read a book, listen to an audiobook, take a CE course, learn a new skill on KWConnect, attend a conference, achieve a certification. *BOLD LAW: Your business grows to the extent that you do.*

"People do not decide their future, they decide their habits and their habits decide their future"

- F. Matthias Alexander

THINGS I
DID WELL

WHAT YOU FOCUS ON EXPANDS

THINGS I LEARNED

THINGS I
DID WELL

COMPLAINING = GARBAGE MAGNET

THINGS I
LEARNED

THINGS I DID WELL

CHANGE THE WAY YOU LOOK AT THINGS AND THE THINGS YOU LOOK AT CHANGE

THINGS I
LEARNED

THINGS I
DID WELL

THINGS I
LEARNED

THINGS I
DID WELL

BE. DO. HAVE.

THINGS I
LEARNED

THINGS I
DID WELL

THERE IS NO TRY

THINGS I
LEARNED

THINGS I
DID WELL

THINGS I LEARNED

THINGS I
DID WELL

WHAT YOU FOCUS ON EXPANDS

THINGS I
LEARNED

THINGS I
DID WELL

COMPLAINING = GARBAGE MAGNET

THINGS I
LEARNED

THINGS I
DID WELL

WANT = LACK

THINGS I
LEARNED

THINGS I
DID WELL

COME FROM CONTRIBUTION

THINGS I LEARNED

THINGS I
DID WELL

DO WHAT YOU HAVE ALWAYS DONE, AND YOU WILL GET
WHAT YOU HAVE ALWAYS GOTTEN

THINGS I
LEARNED

THINGS I DID WELL

IF IT IS NOT ON YOUR SCHEDULE, IT DOESN'T EXIST

THINGS I
LEARNED

THINGS I DID WELL

YOU CAN HAVE REASONS OR RESULTS, AND
YOU CAN'T HAVE BOTH.

THINGS I
LEARNED

THINGS I
DID WELL

ALL WORK EXPANDS TO FILL THE TIME ALLOWED

THINGS I
LEARNED

THINGS I
DID WELL

SUCCESS IS SIMPLE, NOT EASY

THINGS I
LEARNED

THINGS I DID WELL

KEEP YOUR EMOTIONS BETWEEN THE LINES

THINGS I
LEARNED

THINGS I
DID WELL

DON'T MISTAKE MOVEMENT FOR ACHIEVEMENT

THINGS I
LEARNED

THINGS I
DID WELL

THINGS I
LEARNED

THINGS I
DID WELL

CLARITY IS POWER

THINGS I
LEARNED

THINGS I
DID WELL

IT'S NOT ABOUT SELLING REAL ESTATE, IT'S ABOUT
FOLLOWING A SCHEDULE

THINGS I
LEARNED

THINGS I DID WELL

PEOPLE WILL GROW INTO THE CONVERSATIONS YOU CREATE AROUND THEM

THINGS I LEARNED

THINGS I
DID WELL

CHANGE YOUR THINKING – CHANGE YOUR WORLD

THINGS I LEARNED

THINGS I
DID WELL

DON'T COMPARE YOUR INSIDES TO
OTHER PEOPLE'S OUTSIDES

THINGS I
LEARNED

THINGS I
DID WELL

THINGS I
LEARNED

THINGS I
DID WELL

FOCUS ON THE PLAN, NOT THE PROBLEM

THINGS I LEARNED

THINGS I DID WELL

LOGIC MAKES YOU THINK, EMOTIONS MAKE YOU ACT

THINGS I LEARNED

THINGS I DID WELL

THINGS I LEARNED

THINGS I DID WELL

THINGS I LEARNED

THINGS I
DID WELL

THINGS AREN'T ALWAYS HOW THEY APPEAR TO BE

THINGS I LEARNED

THINGS I
DID WELL

THINGS I LEARNED

THINGS I
DID WELL

YOU TEACH PEOPLE HOW TO TREAT YOU

THINGS I LEARNED

THINGS I
DID WELL

SPONTANEITY IS A CONDITIONED REFLEX

THINGS I
LEARNED

THINGS I DID WELL

HOW YOU PARTICIPATE IN HERE IS HOW YOU PARTICIPATE EVERYWHERE

THINGS I
LEARNED

THINGS I
DID WELL

THE PURPOSE OF BUSINESS IS TO FUND A PERFECT LIFE

THINGS I
LEARNED

THINGS I DID WELL

YOU GET WHAT YOU DESERVE IN YOUR IMAGINATION

THINGS I
LEARNED

THINGS I
DID WELL

BE. DO. ACHIEVE.

THINGS I LEARNED

THINGS I
DID WELL

WHAT YOU FOCUS ON EXPANDS

THINGS I LEARNED

THINGS I DID WELL

COMPLAINING = GARBAGE MAGNET

THINGS I
LEARNED

THINGS I
DID WELL

CHANGE THE WAY YOU LOOK AT THINGS AND THE THINGS
YOU LOOK AT CHANGE

THINGS I
LEARNED

THINGS I
DID WELL

THINGS I
LEARNED

THINGS I DID WELL

THINGS I
LEARNED

THINGS I
DID WELL

THERE IS NO TRY

THINGS I
LEARNED

THINGS I
DID WELL

DON'T LISTEN TO YOUR DRUNK MONKEY

THINGS I
LEARNED

THINGS I
DID WELL

WHAT YOU FOCUS ON EXPANDS

THINGS I LEARNED

THINGS I
DID WELL

COMPLAINING = GARBAGE MAGNET

THINGS I
LEARNED

THINGS I DID WELL

WANT = LACK

THINGS I LEARNED

THINGS I
DID WELL

COME FROM CONTRIBUTION

THINGS I
LEARNED

THINGS I
DID WELL

DO WHAT YOU HAVE ALWAYS DONE, AND YOU WILL GET
WHAT YOU HAVE ALWAYS GOTTEN

THINGS I
LEARNED

THINGS I
DID WELL

IF IT IS NOT ON YOUR SCHEDULE, IT DOESN'T EXIST

THINGS I
LEARNED

THINGS I
DID WELL

YOU CAN HAVE REASONS OR RESULTS, AND
YOU CAN'T HAVE BOTH.

THINGS I
LEARNED

THINGS I
DID WELL

ALL WORK EXPANDS TO FILL THE TIME ALLOWED

THINGS I LEARNED

THINGS I
DID WELL

SUCCESS IS SIMPLE, NOT EASY

THINGS I
LEARNED

THINGS I
DID WELL

KEEP YOUR EMOTIONS BETWEEN THE LINES

THINGS I LEARNED

THINGS I
DID WELL

DON'T MISTAKE MOVEMENT FOR ACHIEVEMENT

THINGS I LEARNED

THINGS I
DID WELL

THINGS I
LEARNED

THINGS I
DID WELL

CLARITY IS POWER

THINGS I LEARNED

THINGS I
DID WELL

IT'S NOT ABOUT SELLING REAL ESTATE, IT'S ABOUT
FOLLOWING A SCHEDULE

THINGS I
LEARNED

THINGS I
DID WELL

PEOPLE WILL GROW INTO THE CONVERSATIONS YOU CREATE
AROUND THEM

THINGS I LEARNED

THINGS I
DID WELL

CHANGE YOUR THINKING – CHANGE YOUR WORLD

THINGS I
LEARNED

THINGS I
DID WELL

THINGS I
LEARNED

THINGS I
DID WELL

THINGS I
LEARNED

THINGS I
DID WELL

FOCUS ON THE PLAN, NOT THE PROBLEM

THINGS I
LEARNED

THINGS I DID WELL

LOGIC MAKES YOU THINK, EMOTIONS MAKE YOU ACT

THINGS I LEARNED

THINGS I
DID WELL

NO PRESSURE -- NO DIAMONDS

THINGS I
LEARNED

THINGS I
DID WELL

YOUR CELLS EAVESDROP ON YOUR THOUGHTS

THINGS I LEARNED

THINGS I DID WELL

THINGS AREN'T ALWAYS HOW THEY APPEAR TO BE

THINGS I
LEARNED

THINGS I
DID WELL

YOUR BUSINESS GROWS TO THE EXTENT THAT YOU DO

THINGS I
LEARNED

THINGS I
DID WELL

YOU TEACH PEOPLE HOW TO TREAT YOU

THINGS I LEARNED

THINGS I DID WELL

THINGS I LEARNED

THINGS I
DID WELL

HOW YOU PARTICIPATE IN HERE IS HOW YOU PARTICIPATE
EVERYWHERE

THINGS I
LEARNED

THINGS I
DID WELL

THE PURPOSE OF BUSINESS IS TO FUND A PERFECT LIFE

THINGS I LEARNED

THINGS I
DID WELL

YOU GET WHAT YOU DESERVE IN YOUR IMAGINATION

THINGS I
LEARNED

THINGS I
DID WELL

BE. DO. ACHIEVE.

THINGS I LEARNED

THINGS I
DID WELL

WHAT YOU FOCUS ON EXPANDS

THINGS I
LEARNED

THINGS I
DID WELL

COMPLAINING = GARBAGE MAGNET

THINGS I LEARNED

THINGS I
DID WELL

CHANGE THE WAY YOU LOOK AT THINGS AND THE THINGS
YOU LOOK AT CHANGE

THINGS I
LEARNED

THINGS I
DID WELL

THINGS I LEARNED

THINGS I
DID WELL

BE. DO. HAVE.

THINGS I LEARNED

THINGS I
DID WELL

THERE IS NO TRY

THINGS I
LEARNED

THINGS I
DID WELL

THINGS I
LEARNED

THINGS I
DID WELL

WHAT YOU FOCUS ON EXPANDS

THINGS I
LEARNED

THINGS I DID WELL

COMPLAINING = GARBAGE MAGNET

THINGS I
LEARNED

THINGS I
DID WELL

WANT = LACK

THINGS I LEARNED

THINGS I
DID WELL

COME FROM CONTRIBUTION

THINGS I LEARNED

THINGS I
DID WELL

DO WHAT YOU HAVE ALWAYS DONE, AND YOU WILL GET
WHAT YOU HAVE ALWAYS GOTTEN

THINGS I
LEARNED

THINGS I
DID WELL

IF IT IS NOT ON YOUR SCHEDULE, IT DOESN'T EXIST

THINGS I LEARNED

THINGS I DID WELL

YOU CAN HAVE REASONS OR RESULTS, AND
YOU CAN'T HAVE BOTH.

THINGS I LEARNED

THINGS I DID WELL

ALL WORK EXPANDS TO FILL THE TIME ALLOWED

THINGS I
LEARNED

THINGS I
DID WELL

SUCCESS IS SIMPLE, NOT EASY

THINGS I
LEARNED

THINGS I
DID WELL

THINGS I
LEARNED

THINGS I
DID WELL

DON'T MISTAKE MOVEMENT FOR ACHIEVEMENT

THINGS I
LEARNED

THINGS I
DID WELL

THINGS I LEARNED

THINGS I
DID WELL

CLARITY IS POWER

THINGS I
LEARNED

THINGS I DID WELL

IT'S NOT ABOUT SELLING REAL ESTATE, IT'S ABOUT
FOLLOWING A SCHEDULE

THINGS I LEARNED

THINGS I
DID WELL

PEOPLE WILL GROW INTO THE CONVERSATIONS YOU CREATE
AROUND THEM

THINGS I
LEARNED

THINGS I
DID WELL

CHANGE YOUR THINKING – CHANGE YOUR WORLD

THINGS I
LEARNED

THINGS I
DID WELL

DON'T COMPARE YOUR INSIDES TO
OTHER PEOPLE'S OUTSIDES

THINGS I LEARNED

THINGS I
DID WELL

THINGS I LEARNED

THINGS I
DID WELL

FOCUS ON THE PLAN, NOT THE PROBLEM

THINGS I LEARNED

THINGS I DID WELL

LOGIC MAKES YOU THINK, EMOTIONS MAKE YOU ACT

THINGS I
LEARNED

THINGS I
DID WELL

NO PRESSURE – NO DIAMONDS

THINGS I LEARNED

THINGS I
DID WELL

YOUR CELLS EAVESDROP ON YOUR THOUGHTS

THINGS I
LEARNED

THINGS I
DID WELL

THINGS AREN'T ALWAYS HOW THEY APPEAR TO BE

THINGS I LEARNED

THINGS I
DID WELL

YOUR BUSINESS GROWS TO THE EXTENT THAT YOU DO

THINGS I
LEARNED

THINGS I
DID WELL

YOU TEACH PEOPLE HOW TO TREAT YOU

THINGS I LEARNED

THINGS I DID WELL

SPONTANEITY IS A CONDITIONED REFLEX

THINGS I
LEARNED

THINGS I
DID WELL

HOW YOU PARTICIPATE IN HERE IS HOW YOU PARTICIPATE
EVERYWHERE

THINGS I
LEARNED

THINGS I
DID WELL

THE PURPOSE OF BUSINESS IS TO FUND A PERFECT LIFE

THINGS I
LEARNED

THINGS I
DID WELL

YOU GET WHAT YOU DESERVE IN YOUR IMAGINATION

THINGS I LEARNED

THINGS I
DID WELL

BE. DO. ACHIEVE.

THINGS I LEARNED

Made in the USA
Las Vegas, NV
03 June 2021

24111172R10125